FLYING with FEATHERS and WINGS

CAITIE MCANENEY

PowerKiDS press.
New York

Published in 2018 by The Rosen Publishing Group, Inc.
29 East 21st Street, New York, NY 10010

Copyright © 2018 by The Rosen Publishing Group, Inc.

All rights reserved. No part of this book may be reproduced in any form without permission in writing from the publisher, except by a reviewer.

First Edition

Editor: Elizabeth Krajnik
Book Design: Reann Nye

Photo Credits: Cover, p. 1 Nejron Photo/Shutterstock.com; p. 5 (large flying fox) aDam Wildlife/Shutterstock.com; p. 5 (bee hummingbird) Wang LiQiang/Shutterstock.com; p. 5 (white witch moth) https://commons.wikimedia.org/wiki/File:Thysania_agrippina_0001b_L.D.jpg; p. 6 Daniel Eskridge/Stocktrek Images/Getty Images; p. 7 Education Images/Universal Images Group/Getty Images; p. 8 HIRAN NANCHIANG/Shutterstock.com; p. 9 Lou Cannon/Shutterstock.com; p. 10 robert mcgillivray/Shutterstock.com; p. 11 Brenda Smith DVM/Shutterstock.com; p. 13 Robert L Kothenbeutel/Shutterstock.com; p. 14 digidreamgrafix/Shutterstock.com; p. 15 Alan Jeffery/Shutterstock.com; p. 16 Ian Duffield/Shutterstock.com; p. 17 scooperdigital/Shutterstock.com; p. 18 Martens Tom/Shutterstock.com; p. 19 Daan Kloeg/Shutterstock.com; p. 20 Natural Earth Imagery/Shutterstock.com; p. 21 Martin Mecnarowski/Shutterstock.com; p. 22 Auscape/Universal Images Group/Getty Images.

Cataloging-in-Publication Data

Names: McAneney, Caitie.
Title: Flying with feathers and wings / Caitie McAneney.
Description: New York : PowerKids Press, 2018. | Series: How animals adapt to survive | Includes index.
Identifiers: ISBN 9781538328392 (pbk.) | ISBN 9781508164340 (library bound) | ISBN 9781538328453 (6 pack)
Subjects: LCSH: Feathers–Juvenile literature. | Wings (Anatomy)–Juvenile literature. | Birds–Flight–Juvenile literature.
Classification: LCC QL697.4 M286 2018 | DDC 598.147–dc23

Manufactured in the United States of America

CONTENTS

The GIFT of FLIGHT............4
PREHISTORIC BIRD...............6
FANTASTIC FEATHERS............8
WONDERFUL WINGS.............10
HOVERING HUMMINGBIRDS......12
PRETTY PARROTS...............14
OWL SUPERPOWERS............16
ARCTIC ADVENTURERS..........18
DEEP DIVERS...................20
FLYING into the FUTURE........22
GLOSSARY.......................23
INDEX..........................24
WEBSITES......................24

The GIFT of FLIGHT

Why do birds have wings? Why do turtles have shells? Why do chameleons change color? The answer is adaptation. Over millions of years, animals have adapted, or changed, to survive in their **environment**. Some adaptations, such as **camouflage**, keep animals safe from predators, while others, such as fins and flippers, help animals move from one place to another.

Some animals with wings have the amazing ability of flight. These animals include not only birds but bats, butterflies, and bees. All birds also have feathers, which help them fly, keep them warm, and attract **mates**. Feathered flying animals include parrots, hummingbirds, and owls.

> An animal's wingspan is the distance from the tip of one wing to the tip of the other wing. If a human were a bird, their wingspan would have to be very large.

IMPRESSIVE WINGSPANS

WANDERING ALBATROSS
LONGEST BIRD WINGSPAN
11 feet (3.35 m)

male BEE HUMMINGBIRD
SHORTEST BIRD WINGSPAN
1.2 inches (3 cm)

WHITE WITCH MOTH
LONGEST INSECT WINGSPAN
11 inches (28 cm)

TANZANIAN PARASITIC WASP
SHORTEST INSECT WINGSPAN
0.0079 inches (0.2 mm)

LARGE FLYING FOX
LONGEST BAT WINGSPAN
4 feet 11 inches (1.5 m)

BUMBLEBEE BAT
SHORTEST BAT WINGSPAN
6.3 inches (16 cm)

PREHISTORIC BIRD

The first flying creatures on Earth were insects. They ruled the air without competition for many years. Then, some reptiles **developed** the ability to fly. These creatures are called pterosaurs. This group included *Pterodactylus* and *Quetzalcoatlus*. Their wings were not made of feathers. Instead, they were made of skin stretched between their fingers and their legs. Members of this group of predators lived on Earth for about 140 million years.

Adaptation Answers

Some scientists believe that the creature from which birds evolved didn't appear until after all the dinosaurs had died out—about 65 million years ago. Scientists are still on the lookout for more proof that birds evolved during the dinosaurs' lifetime.

We can learn a lot about bird **ancestors** through fossils. Scientists use fossils to make images of what prehistoric creatures actually looked like.

In 2015, two scientists discovered 130-million-year-old fossils of two **prehistoric** birds. These birds, named *Archaeornithura meemannae*, look more like modern birds than previous discoveries suggested. It is likely that modern birds **evolved** from *Archaeornithura*.

FANTASTIC FEATHERS

Why did creatures develop feathers? Some feathered animals, such as peacocks, use colorful feathers to attract mates. Others, such as owls, use feathers to blend in with their surroundings.

Adaptation Answers

The first feathered animals likely didn't fly. That leads scientists to believe that feathers were probably first used to appeal to mates and keep creatures warm in colder weather.

SMOOTH REGION

CONTOUR FEATHER

DOWNY REGION

Contour feathers overlap on a bird's body like shingles on a roof. These are the feathers we see.

While not all feathered creatures can fly, many have that ability. The way birds' feathers are arranged is perfect for flight. Feathers are light and **flexible**, and they allow birds to cut through the air.

Birds have a layer of down, or light and fluffy feathers close to the bird's body. They also have contour feathers, which have a downy region. These feathers prevent heat from leaving and cold from entering the bird's body, keeping it warm even in very cold weather.

WONDERFUL WINGS

Winged reptiles used their wings for flight, just as many of today's birds do. Flight gives animals a greater ability to move from place to place over long or short distances. They can fly over water to find new places to live or perch high in trees where other animals won't bother their nest. Some birds use flight to hunt and swoop down on their prey.

Adaptation Answers

A bird's wingspan tells us a lot about what the bird uses its wings for. The albatross uses its huge, strong wings to fly long distances over open water.

This golden eagle has a wingspan of 6 to 7.5 feet (1.8 to 2.2 m). Its wingspan helps it soar high in the sky.

Each bird species, or kind, has a different kind of wing. The smallest bird wingspan is 1.2 inches (3 cm) and belongs to the male bee hummingbird. The largest wingspan is around 11 feet (3.35 m) and belongs to the wandering albatross.

HOVERING HUMMINGBIRDS

Hummingbirds have some of the smallest wingspans of all birds. These tiny birds don't need a long wingspan to fly from place to place. Unlike the albatross and other seabirds, hummingbirds use their wings for fast bursts of flying and **hovering** over flowers.

Some hummingbird species can beat their wings more than 5,000 times per minute as they hover. They drink nectar from one flower and then speed off to the next one. Their wings move so fast they make a humming sound. Some hummingbirds can fly faster than 30 miles (48.3 km) an hour. Their tiny, flexible wings enable them to fly both forward and backward.

Adaptation Answers

Hummingbirds have adapted to be as light and quick as possible. Many weigh less than a nickel.

Hummingbirds are built for flying, not walking. Their feet are quite weak and tiny, so they tend to only perch and fly.

PRETTY PARROTS

There are more than 350 species in the group of birds called parrots, including cockatoos, parakeets, and macaws. Parrots have four toes on each foot, which is an adaptation that helps them grasp tree branches. Many parrots, especially macaws, are known for their colorful feathers.

Adaptation Answers

Parrots are social creatures. That means they love to fly and perch with a flock of other parrots. Living and working together is another adaptation.

Macaws have bright, long tail feathers. These feathers, along with feathers in the wings, are sometimes called flight feathers. They help the bird steer as it flies.

A macaw's bright feathers are an adaptation for life in the rain forest. Their wings often have red, blue, green, and yellow feathers. They have long, colorful tail feathers, too. The rain forest is full of bright, colorful flowers, trees, and fruits. Thanks to these colorful feathers, macaws blend into their rain forest environment.

OWL SUPERPOWERS

Owls are nighttime hunters. They fly in the dark, finding their prey with special senses. They have an amazing sense of sight, and they use their big eyes to find prey in the dark.

Most owl species have adapted to blend in with their surroundings. That keeps prey from spotting them during a hunt.

They also have a great sense of hearing, thanks in part to their feathers. Owl faces have an interesting adaptation. Their face feathers are shaped like two dishes. The shape gathers sound and directs it straight to the owl's ears. Unlike humans, owls can hear even the quietest sounds. Owls have also developed wide, short wings. This wing shape helps them fly between the trees in a forest.

ARCTIC ADVENTURERS

Engineers **design** jets to be aerodynamic, which means they move through the air easily. The nose of a jet is usually pointed, and the wings are long and thin. That kind of design is similar to the body and wing shape of the amazing Arctic tern.

The Arctic tern has adapted to its long **migrations** over time. This bird holds the record for the longest migration of any animal in the world. Each year, the Arctic tern travels between Greenland in the north and Antarctica in the south, a distance of about 44,000 miles (70,811.1 km).

Arctic terns can live for around 30 years. That means they make the across-the-world trip dozens of times.

19

DEEP DIVERS

Some birds use their wings not to fly but to swim. Perhaps the most well-known swimming birds are penguins. Over time, penguins' wings have developed into flat flippers. They can no longer fly like other birds, but they can dive into the water to catch fish.

Penguin flippers are a great example of bird wings adapting based on their surroundings.

Adaptation Answers

Penguin feathers are an adaptation. They use their smooth feathers to slide on their belly across ice and snow. Their feathers also help keep them warm in the cold.

The puffin is a bird that uses its wings to both fly and swim. Those abilities are necessary because it spends most of its life at sea. While puffins are underwater, they hunt small fish up to 200 feet (61 m) deep. While in the air, the puffin can fly up to 55 miles (88.5 km) an hour.

FLYING into the FUTURE

Research suggests that there are about 18,000 species, or kinds, of birds in the world. In addition to birds, there are thousands of species of winged insects, different species of bats, and even species of winged reptiles!

Draco volans, or the common flying dragon, has adapted a set of ribs that it can stick out to protect itself from its predators. When the lizard puffs its ribs out, the skin between the ribs stretches, acting like wings. These reptiles can't fly, but their "wings" catch the wind, allowing them to glide. In the future, more amazing animals like the *Draco volans* may be discovered!

GLOSSARY

ancestor: An animal that lived before others in its family tree.

camouflage: Colors or shapes on animals that allow them to blend in with their surroundings.

design: To create a plan for something.

develop: The act of changing over time.

environment: The conditions that surround a living thing and affect the way it lives.

evolve: To grow and change over millions of years.

flexible: Capable of bending or being bent.

hover: To float in the air without moving much.

mate: One of two animals that come together to produce babies.

migration: The movement of animals from one place to another as the seasons change.

prehistoric: Having to do with the time before written history.

INDEX

A
albatross, 5, 10, 11, 12
Antarctica, 18
Archaeornithura meemannae, 7
Arctic tern, 18, 19

B
bat, 4, 5, 22
bee, 4
bee hummingbird, 5, 11
bird, 4, 5, 6, 7, 9, 10, 11, 12, 14, 15, 18, 20, 21, 22
bumblebee bat, 5
butterfly, 4

C
cockatoo, 14
contour feathers, 9

D
dinosaur, 6
down, 9
Draco volans, 22

F
flying fox, 5
fossils, 7

G
golden eagle, 11
Greenland, 18

H
hummingbird, 4, 5, 11, 12, 13

I
insect, 5, 6, 22

M
macaw, 14, 15
migration, 18
moth, 5

O
owl, 4, 8, 16, 17

P
parakeet, 14
parrot, 4, 14
peacock, 8
penguin, 20
Pterodactylus, 6
pterosaurs, 6
puffin, 21

Q
Quetzalcoatlus, 6

R
reptile, 6, 10, 22

T
Tanzanian parasitic wasp, 5

W
wandering albatross, 5, 11
white witch moth, 5
wingspan, 4, 5, 10, 11, 12

WEBSITES

Due to the changing nature of Internet links, PowerKids Press has developed an online list of websites related to the subject of this book. This site is updated regularly. Please use this link to access the list: www.powerkidslinks.com/haas/wing